Mary's Crescent

A four day walk from Portchester Castle to Chichester Cathedral, through the South Downs National Park, exploring medieval churches dedicated to St Mary.

Dr Tim Goulder
Illustrated by Simon Privett

ISBN 978 1 84674 417 4

All materials used in the manufacture of this book carry FSC certification.

PUBLISHED BY COUNTRYSIDE BOOKS, NEWBURY
PRODUCED BY THE LETTERWORKS LTD., READING
TYPESET BY KT DESIGNS, ST HELENS
PRINTED BY HOLYWELL PRESS, OXFORD

ACKNOWLEDGEMENTS

I dedicate this book to Saint Mary – the Blessed Virgin Mary.

I would like to express my grateful thanks to my wife Veronica, her unstinted support has made this guide possible. Also to Professor Eamon Duffy and Sir Roy Strong who have allowed me to quote from their books, *The Stripping of the Altars* and A *Little History of the English Country Church* respectively.

Thanks also to Monsignor Jeremy Garrett for advice on Mary's Dowry and to my family and friends who have accompanied me on the walks and given encouragement and helpful advice, particularly my son Chris for his invaluable help with the photography and images, and my son in law, Cass, for creating the website.

Simon Privett accompanied me on the Camino de Santiago, where I saw at first hand his delightful church drawings. He has diligently drawn all the Mary churches on this walk and sketched some of the interior features I refer to in the commentary, for which I am very grateful.

All proceeds from this publication will go to support the fabric of the seven St Mary churches and Chichester Cathedral.

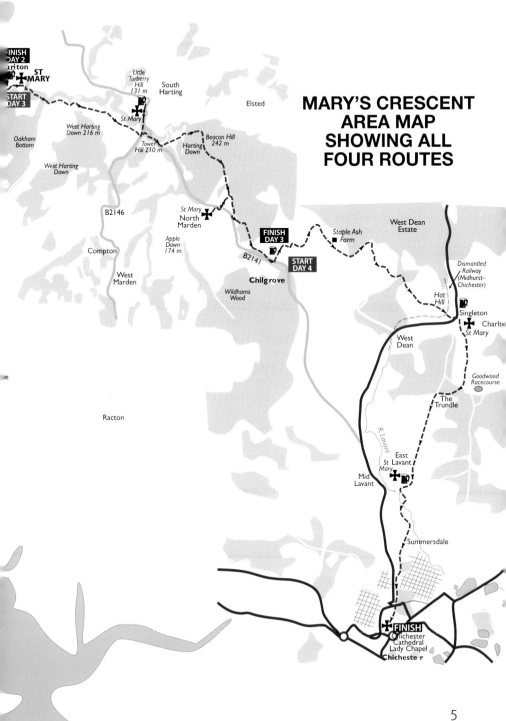

A3 (M)

FINISH
DAY 2
Triton
ST
MARY

START
DAY 3

Little
Torberry
Hill
131 m

South
Harting

Elsted

St Mary

West Harting
Down 216 m

Oakham
Bottom

Tower
Hill 210 m

Harting
Down

Beacon Hill
242 m

West Harting
Down

MARY'S CRESCENT
AREA MAP
SHOWING ALL
FOUR ROUTES

B2146

St Mary
North
Marden

FINISH
DAY 3

Staple Ash
■ Farm

West Dean
Estate

Apple
Down
174 m

B2141

START
DAY 4

Dismantled
Railway
(Midhurst–
Chichester)

Compton

Chilgrove

Hat
Hill

Singleton

West
Marden

Wildhams
Wood

Charlt
St Mary

West
Dean

Goodwood
Racecourse

Racton

The
Trundle

R. Lavant

East
St Lavant
Mary

Mid
Lavant

Summersdale

FINISH
Chichester
Cathedral
Lady Chapel
Chichester

5

CONTENTS

INTRODUCTION

Great Britain has a wealth of ancient medieval churches and southern England is no exception; churches built by our Saxon and Norman forbears commonly nestle within the spectacular countryside of the South Downs.

England was renowned in the Middle Ages for being "Mary's dowry"*. The sense that England had been given to Mary and was her treasured possession was a catalyst for devotion to the Blessed Virgin Mary – St Mary. This largely disappeared after the Reformation and has remained quiescent ever since.

The churches that form the skeleton of this four day walk demonstrate the breadth and wealth of ancient ecclesiastical architecture present since the early Middle Ages – from the Priory Church of Portchester to the great English Cathedral at Chichester, with the simple single-celled church of North Marden and the Norman gems of Droxford, Buriton, South Harting, Singleton and East Lavant in-between.

The Walk Guide

This guide gives a detailed description of each day's walk and a brief description of the churches to be visited, emphasizing features still present from the medieval period that were important elements to worship at that time, but ceased to have a role post Reformation.

I chose to start the walk at St Mary's Portchester, walking eastward and finishing at the Mary Chapel of Chichester Cathedral. The final day is rewarded by views over the Solent, with Chichester Cathedral lying below and the Isle of Wight beyond, and if your timing is right – sung evensong at the Cathedral.

Portchester has free car parking and also has a railway station, however it lacks suitable accommodation. This means it is easier to start your walk in the morning at Portchester and arrive on the final afternoon at Chichester. There is a direct train from Chichester to Portchester for those needing to collect their car.

* See page 33

Why Mary's Crescent?

With the ancient Marian devotion in mind and a love of the spectacular local countryside I decided, prior to this Millennium, to explore the pre-Reformation churches dedicated to St Mary within a 20 mile radius of where I live, combining the visits with a circular walk from the church and a lunchtime visit to the local pub.

However in 2010, accompanied by two friends, I began walking the pilgrim route from St Jean Pied de Port in western France, east of the Pyrenees, to Santiago de Compostela in north-west Spain. We took a week or two out of the following four years to complete the journey; the daily rhythm of walking, companionship and reflection made me wonder if some of the churches I had explored near my home could be combined into a few days' walk.

Whilst studying the OS maps of my local area it became clear that the 45-mile walk from Portchester northwards through the Meon Valley, east over the South Downs and finally south to Chichester could conveniently be segmented into four days, each day beginning and ending near a medieval church dedicated to St Mary. And so the genesis of this modern pilgrim route was conceived, the geographical crescent shape suggesting the guide's title too – Mary's Crescent.

Website

www.maryscrescent.com

Use the website to download OS and GPX files for:
1 Each day's walk
2 Cycle routes between St Mary churches
3 Short circular walks from each individual St Mary church

Medieval churches

Striking as these churches are today, their present day interiors differ markedly from those in the centuries prior to the Reformation. As I walked through the churchyard to the entrance of each church I tried to imagine how it might have been over 500 years ago, what now remains of the medieval interior and in what way did the church now reflect its original dedication.

Church worship in the Middle Ages

In medieval times village and parish life coalesced in ceremonies throughout the year; Holy Days, Saints' Days, the turning points of the seasons – Winter Solstice, Easter and Spring – all enacted in the church and sometimes in the churchyard. Events involved processions, music, singing and dance. In effect the Holy Mass (the Christian service celebrated in medieval churches) enabled the integration of people, parish and worship through liturgy (the form of the Christian service), feast days and processions.

Any substantial parish would have a cluster of gilds (modern spelling – guilds) each with their own patron saint, mass celebrations and processions. Gilds were a fraternity of local parishioners devoted to a particular saint (for example the Blessed Virgin Mary) or aspect of Christian veneration (for example Corpus Christi – the body of Christ). The gilds honoured their saint during Mass by lighting candles, providing prayers for deceased members of the gild, promoting charity and a sense of local community through alms given to the poor and with feast days – when food and ale would be given to local parishioners following the gild Mass.

There was no secular sense of time; everything – legal deeds, anniversaries for birthdays, leases and rent – were all related to the liturgical calendar of Holy Days.

Rood supported on a rood beam, Holy Cross Church, Kaysersberg, Alsace

Holy Mass was a celebration people participated in rather than sought to comprehend – the central event was the transubstantiation of the host (an oval bread wafer) into Christ's actual body, and wine into his blood. Believers did not view this as a symbolic change, but the real change of the substance of bread and wine. The bread and wine were thus "consecrated" and were then called the "blessed sacraments". This action, which in effect confirmed Christ's power to save a soul from damnation, was enhanced and focused by the interior architecture of the church chancel and nave, and especially its interface at the chancel arch. To participate meant only to see the host raised by the priest at the point of its transformation and in the late medieval period parishioners might partake in this event several times a day.

Worship included the concept of Purgatory – the place where the dead could be redeemed from their sins. Redemption was dependent on the living (relatives, parishioners and fellow guildsmen) ensuring Mass was said for the soul of the dead. Redemption was aided by the belief that good works and gifts to adorn the church or beautify its worship were also efficacious.

The role of the parish church was not just worship, but also patronage. Private and Chantry chapels*, tombs, monuments, images, crosses and devotional ornaments – paid for by the parishioners – would on a daily basis commemorate saints as well as past parishioners' family members, all within the overarching context of the Christian world represented by the Rood – a life-size painted figure of Christ on the cross with Saints Mary and John kneeling by. It was erected across the chancel arch (Rood is the Anglo-Saxon word for a cross) supported on an oak Rood beam and beneath the Rood would be an elaborate wooden screen – the Rood screen.

Professor Eamon Duffy vividly describes the changes that took place in churches from pre- and post-Reformation in his book *The Stripping of the Altars*.

He comments, *"the overwhelming impression left by sources for late medieval religion in England is that of a Christianity resolutely and enthusiastically orientated towards the public and the corporate, and of a continuing sense of the value of cooperation and mutuality in seeking salvation."*

Today, when visiting sparse churchyards and empty churches, it is

* See page 34

difficult to imagine the spectacle, theatre and spiritual momentum created by these events.

A good example is Palm Sunday (the Sunday before Easter). The village parishioners would congregate in the church for a blessing and sprinkling of holy water followed by the reading from Saint John's Gospel of Christ's entry to Jerusalem. The congregation would then process outside to a large wooden cross erected in the churchyard, all the while the choir singing anthems. In the meantime a mobile shrine with a silk canopy holding the blessed sacrament and the church's precious relics (for example bone or hair from saints – which acted as spiritual catalysts), processed towards the parish congregation. Further anthems were sung and the two processions then combined to walk around the church passing a scaffold erected on the south wall, which enabled choirboys to sing and flowers and unconsecrated wafers to be strewn before the blessed sacrament in the mobile shrine. From there the procession would return into the church, passing beneath the canopy of the shrine, ending in front of the Rood – the most important focal point of the medieval church, but now absent from all English churches.

The congregation stood in front of the Rood screen, above was the Rood covered by a veil. The veil would be raised revealing the life-size statue of the crucified Jesus. At this all the parishioners would kneel and the clergy would venerate the cross by kissing the ground before it. The Passion story would then be sung or read from the Rood loft, a balcony beside the Rood.

Through the Middle Ages, as the population grew, concern about the use of wealth to place before God a permanent witness to their piety and charity, led to donations for the expansion of churches – chancels and naves were lengthened, north and south aisles were added to house additional chapels and altars; bell towers were built. There would have been an abundance of Saints' images, and in churches dedicated to St Mary, statues of Mary and the infant Jesus. There would be wall paintings, painted glass and numerous altars in the nave as well as the main altar at the east end of the chancel.

As Sir Roy Strong says –

> "...to comprehend the importance of images we need to understand the medieval mindset... virtually the only images

he or she ever saw were displayed in the parish church: the statue of the Virgin over the porch, the interior depicting stories from the bible, the Last Judgement or Doom, and images of the virgin and the saints. There would also be sculpted figures of the Rood and those of saints attached to various altars. As stained glass became more common from the twelfth century, the windows too were a phantasmagoria of images."

At the Reformation, instigated in 1536 during the reign of Henry VIII, the process of destroying everything associated with the Catholic Mass began; altars were destroyed, walls whitewashed, painted glass smashed, statues removed or decapitated, roods and rood lofts dismantled; altar clothes, priestly vestments and candles banned – along with most feast and holy days.

Architectural features associated with church worship in the Middle Ages

1. Church and Churchyard

On entering a churchyard in the medieval period there would have been few if any gravestones, the consecrated (holy) space would be dominated by a cross, sometimes of stone, more often of wood – the focal point of religious ceremonies.

A Saxon church consisted of a simple rectangular Nave and Chancel, with the Chancel facing eastwards. The Chancel was smaller than the Nave and the wall of the east end would be semi-circular (known as apse). Through the 11th to 15th centuries the buildings were altered by the addition of south and north aisles, remodelling of the chancel east end to replace the apse with a flat wall and enlarged east window, finally the addition of a tower and south porch. In the churches you will visit some of these developments are obvious, in others (such as North Marden) very little change has occurred.

The following elements of the church would have been commonplace in any medieval church, and many are still visible in the churches you will visit. Others – such as the Rood and Rood screen – have been obliterated.

At the Reformation "The Stripping of the Altars" was literally true; altars were removed, leaving one table in the centre of the chancel rather than at the east end. Out went all internal adornment, saints' images, candles, the pyx, painted glass, rood, rood stair and loft.

2. Porch

The porch was where village business and marriages were conducted – the interface between the secular and heavenly worlds. Over the entrance there would have been a statue of the Virgin Mary (as in St Mary Singleton where a statue niche still exists).

To quote Sir Roy Strong:

> "the porch was the gateway to Christian life. Moreover, we know from the later Middle Ages how important the porch

Porch with stoup and blocked statue niche – St Mary Singleton

was: it was here that business was transacted, oaths sworn, bargains struck, disputes settled, marriages solemnized and part of the baptismal rite conducted."

3. Scratch (Mass) Dials

Mass dials are found on the south-facing wall of many medieval churches. Their purpose was to mark the time of liturgical services through the day. They are about the size of a side plate and consisted of a simple indicator (called a gnomon), usually a wooden peg, which fitted into a central hole drilled into the wall, with an outer arc where radial lines marked the time of church services. When the sun shone the priest would place the peg in the wall and when

Scratch (Mass) Dial – St Mary Droxford

15

Stoup – St Mary Singleton

the shadow cast by the peg fell across a radial line, the service would commence.

There are four dials inscribed on the south wall of Droxford church.

4. Stoup

A basin for holy water, usually on the wall near the porch for worshippers to dip their fingers in before crossing themselves, as a reminder of the cleansing from sin they received at their own baptism. An example is on the outer wall of the porch, to the right of the doorway, at St Mary Singleton.

5. Nave, Chancel and Rood

Within the church, the chancel (symbolically heaven) and nave (symbolically earth) were separated by the chancel arch.

Suspended from the arch, or resting on the beam across the arch, would be the Rood – a life-sized crucifix bearing Christ.

The life-size crucifix supported on a beam would have dominated the church.

6. Rood screen and stair

During the 13th century rood screens began to be built. They made more obvious the separation of the nave and chancel and their purpose was to enhance the spiritual experience and holy mystery of the Mass. They were the visual showpiece of the parish church and the most important investment by the parishioners. To quote Eamon Duffy, *"The screen itself was both a barrier and no barrier.*

Painted rood chancel screen – St Edmund's Southwold

Stone chancel screen – Chichester Cathedral

It was not a wall but rather a set of windows, a frame for liturgical drama."

Usually built in wood, occasionally in stone and highly decorated, the rood screen filled the space created by the chancel arch. At the base of the screen would be a solid wooden beam, above this a painted dado screen, then wooden arches and tracery supporting the rood beam, which carried the statues of the Virgin Mary and Saint John the Evangelist placed either side of the crucifix bearing Christ (the Rood). Sometimes there would be additional figures depicting apostles, angels, saints and benefactors.

In some churches, especially in the later medieval period, when the church was refurbished, a standing area called a rood loft was developed above the screen; the rood beam and figures could be incorporated in this or the beam could be set above the loft.

In both St Mary's Droxford and Singleton there still exists the stone staircase to the original but now demolished rood loft – a tribute

Entrance to the Rood loft stair, St Mary Singleton – the Rood, Rood loft, Tympanum and Chancel screen have all been removed.

to the expense the parishes must have gone too to create an impressive rood loft.

Above and behind the Rood, filling in the space of the chancel arch, would be a wooden tympanum (Latin for drum) painted on its west facing surface – towards the nave. Very often with a Doom painting depicting Judgement Day.

By the 13th century the responsibility for the Chancel and Nave had separated – the Chancel was the priest's and the Nave the parishioners'. This precipitated a spree of spending on the Nave by wealthy parishioners to create chapels dedicated to gilds or families – with associated saints depicted in figures, wall paintings and on painted chapel wooden screens; alongside burning candles the whole effect would have provided an astonishing contrast to the outside world.

The Lateran (or Papal) Council of 1215 instructed Bishops to encourage devotion and piety, this influenced church rood screen painting as well as wall paintings and stained glass.

In 1561 a Royal Order by Elizabeth I ordered rood lofts to be taken down, and if the rood screen remained it was to have the royal crest on it – usually the royal coat of arms. The order also required churches to have "a comely partition betwixt the chancel and church". However during the Civil War screens were removed and this continued into the 18th century when they were considered visually intrusive.

7. Font

Fonts have been a feature of the Christian church for 2000 years and are still used for baptizing new Christians. The word baptism comes from the Greek "baptismos" meaning immersion. Water is used, symbolizing cleansing of the spirit.

They are usually made of stone, representing permanence and dignity, and stand in the western end of the nave, often near the porch, where it symbolizes entry into the church.

Elaborate Font – St Mary Portchester

Plain Font – St Mary North Marden

The basins vary in shape from a simple circular, square or octagonal tub requiring only the skills of a local stonemason, to complex sculpted forms with interwoven designs and figures – the sign of wealth and endowment.

All the churches on this pilgrimage have a font, and in all but East Lavant and Droxford they are medieval in origin.

8. Wall paintings

To most medieval people bare unpainted stone surfaces looked unfinished, the walls were usually whitewashed and brightly painted. Religious scenes filled the walls, especially around the altar. Bright colours, simple geometric and floral patterns enriched architectural features such as mouldings, columns and capitals.

From the 13th century onwards the walls would have been adorned with frescoes. These have all gone from the churches I explored apart from St Mary's Buriton where on the low side of the south window of the Chancel is a 13th-century mural of the Virgin

21

Virgin and Child – St Mary Buriton

Vault – Lady Chapel, Chichester Cathedral

Entrance to Treasury, Chichester Cathedral

and Child, and St Mary Droxford, where the remnants of paint can be seen on the east wall of the north chapel. Similar fragments remain in Chichester Cathedral.

9. Painted Glass

Painted glass became increasingly popular through the 13th century onwards. Initially small medallions of coloured glass with images of saints were used, later purely decorative patterns were used, including plain glass to allow more light penetration. Glaziers had to respond to the changing architectural styles, as the simple Norman lancet developed into larger more elaborate Gothic windows.

The medieval stained glass in the churches you will visit were destroyed during the Reformation, however, fragments survived and were reinstated in later years, as in St Mary's North Marden and Singleton.

10. Altar

Following the Lateran Council of 1215, churches were required to have stone altars at the eastern end of the chancel. Each altar was to have five crosses representing the wounds of Christ (hands, feet, chest).

Behind the altar there might be a reredos, an ornamental screen covering the wall at the back of an altar, with tiers of statues. On the ceiling carved angels and images and the surrounding walls would have been painted.

Crammed into the nave, even small churches had their quota of altars for the celebration of gild and chantry masses (mass for the dead). These can be identified by piscinas – see below – that still remain outside the chancel, for example in the north and south chapels at St Mary Droxford. Of particular note, at St Mary South Harting, high up on the south side of the chancel arch is a piscina for celebrating Mass from the now nonexistent Rood loft.

11. Pyx

The Pyx was suspended above and in front of the High Altar, it is a container – usually of silver and covered with costly fabric – for the

Double Aumbry – Lady Chapel Chichester Cathedral

consecrated host which, to the medieval eye, was the actual body of Christ in the form of a wafer; an object of veneration and adoration. These are no longer present in any of the churches you will visit.

12. Aumbry

A recessed cabinet with a wooden door, now usually no longer present, set in the wall of the chancel for storing sacred vessels – for example the chalice. Sometimes placed near the piscina or on the opposite wall of the chancel. There is an example in the north wall of the chancel at St Mary Singleton, St Mary Buriton as well as the Lady Chapel of Chichester Cathedral.

13. Piscina

Several of the churches you will visit have piscinas; these were shallow bowls made of stone and set into the south wall of the chancel near the altar with (usually) a drainage pipe to the earth outside. They are also

Piscina – South Chapel, St Mary Droxford

found outside the chancel where subsidiary chapels were formed for guild or family services.

They were common in churches from the 13th century onwards. Their purpose was to dispose of the water used to clean the cup and plate that held the consecrated bread and wine – not however to drain any of the actual consecrated bread and wine which had to be consumed by the priest. They were also used by the priest to ritually wash his hands prior to the consecration of the host.

14. Easter Sepulchre

In all medieval churches an Easter Sepulchre would have been set up as a focus for the sacred time of Easter week and Easter Sunday, usually made of wood and positioned on the north wall of the chancel.

At the end of the Good Friday service, the Pyx, containing a consecrated host and the cross, which parishioners had venerated by kissing it during the service, were wrapped in linen cloth and placed in the sepulchre that had been erected on the north side of the chancel.

Easter Sepulchre – St Mary East Lavant

The sepulchre was the shape and size of a "hearse", covered with rich and expensive cloth embroidered with scenes from Christ's Passion and donated by wealthy parishioners, the poorer parishioners donating candles. Thus Christ was symbolically buried in the sepulchre in the form of consecrated host inside the pyx.

The only remaining examples today are stone, usually a tomb to commemorate an important parishioner but positioned in the north chancel wall to act as the Easter Sepulchre.

A good example is at St Mary's East Lavant where the stone monument is now positioned on the ground floor of the tower. The stone monument to the Earl of Arundel in the north chancel wall of St Mary Singleton may have served a similar purpose.

15. Misericords (Latin for "mercy" or "pity")

The seats within the medieval choir were hinged so that when upright they revealed a bracket that the standing priest or deacon could rest

27

Misericord – St Mary East Lavant

against. They generally existed in the chapels of religious institutions such as a monastery, cathedral or abbey. Monks were required to stand for long periods of regulated prayer time throughout the day and during the 11th century misericords were introduced to assist the elderly. There is an example at St Mary, East Lavant. Why a parish church would have them is a mystery but in East Lavant's case the church is in the gift of the Archbishop of Canterbury and this may have influenced the endowment.

There are further wonderful examples in the choir of Chichester Cathedral.

16. Sedilia (Latin for "seats")

These are seats, usually of stone and placed in the chancel on the south side of the altar, for use during Mass (the medieval church service) by the officiating priest and his assistants. They are often set back into the main wall of the church itself. The stone work surrounding the recessed

Three-step Sedilia with piscina – St Mary Buriton

seat can be elaborate with canopies and subdivided by shafts. Seats can sometimes be at different levels with the eastern-most being highest.

There are examples in the south chancel wall of St Mary Buriton and the Lady Chapel Chichester Cathedral.

17. Medieval Graffiti

Graffiti are common in pre-formation churches. Today the word "graffiti" often implies mindless vandalism and defacement, but as marks inscribed into the masonry nothing could be further from the truth. The graffiti was inscribed through the plaster onto the stone which would have created a clear and stark image with white stone showing through the painted plasterwork. It was also drawn onto the already painted walls using charcoal or other material.

Only the inscribed graffiti is left today and several examples are present in the churches you will visit. Daisy wheels (hexafoils) and circles were common (St Mary Droxford and Buriton), they are known as "apotropaic" or ritual protection marks. It was thought that demonic influences were attracted to lines, which once entered had to be

"Daisy Wheel" – St Mary Droxford

VV – Virgo Virginum and inverted for M – Mary. – St Mary Buriton
Drill holes in the shape of a cross

Ragged staff – heraldic emblem of the Earls of Warwick, St Mary Singleton

followed to their ends, and as a circle has no end, they are trapped for all time.

Having a similar protective effect, VV marks stood for Virgo Virginum (the virgin of virgins) representing the Virgin Mary. Sometimes the sign is inverted to become M – for Mary (St Mary Buriton).

Drilled holes in the masonry, usually in groups, are thought to indicate that the stone powder produced was taken and used in potions for ailments, thus adding a "holy" power and benefit to the medication (St Mary Buriton). The drill holes are commonly near apotropaic symbols.

Sometimes there are heraldic marks, for example in the porch of St Mary Singleton, or as in Chichester Cathedral cloister, a pattern of holes providing the board for a game of "Nine Men's Morris", is thought to have been carved by pilgrims waiting their turn to pray at the tomb of St Richard.

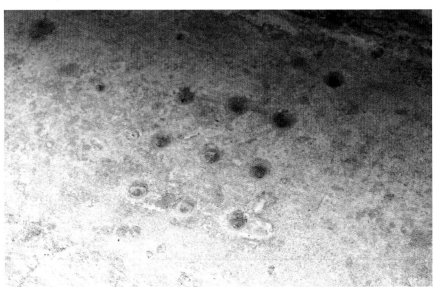

Medieval pastimes: Nine Men's Morris, Chichester Cathedral Cloister

Mary's Dowry

References to Mary's Dowry date back to medieval times. Widespread by the middle of the 14th century, it reflected a deep devotion to Mary (Blessed Virgin Mary) in medieval England and a belief that she took a particular protective interest in England's affairs, acting through her powers of intercession as guardian and defender.

Thomas Arundel (Archbishop of York and later Canterbury during the reigns of Richard II and Henry V) wrote *"we English being... her own Dowry, as we are commonly called, ought to surpass others in the fervour of our praises and devotions"*.

The Wilton Diptych   (Bought with a special grant and contributions from Samuel Courtauld, Viscount Rothermere, C. T. Stoop and the Art Fund, 1929) Copyright The National Gallery

The title dos Mariae, "dowry of Mary", was used in English Latin texts and English priests sought the intercession of "the Virgin, protectress of her dower" on the eve of the Battle of Agincourt.

The famous Wilton Diptych (now in the National Gallery), commissioned by Richard II as a guarantee of his devotion and sincerity, shows the king kneeling, with his patron, St John the Baptist, at his side presenting him to Mary with the saintly English kings, Edward the Confessor and St Edmund the Martyr beside them. Mary listens to their cause and obliges by leaning forward so that her infant son can give his blessing to the king.

Chantry

A chantry was a foundation by which a priest could be employed to say Mass for the soul of an individual or deceased members of a gild in perpetuity. The Mass would be said at a chantry altar and the priest would be called a chantry priest. Land was a common source of investment to provide the necessary income.

A chantry chapel is an enclosed area with a dedicated altar set aside within the church, usually the nave but possibly in the side aisles or transepts. The walls would usually be made of wood and of similar design to the rood screen. They were endowed by individuals or gilds, and the expense of furnishing would reflect the importance of patronage.

OVERVIEW OF THE FOUR-DAY WALK FROM PORTCHESTER TO CHICHESTER

There is no hard and fast rule about the length of each day's journey. The routes I have suggested suited my walking pace and preferred distance, combined with visiting the churches. It means the first two days are more than 12 miles whether you end the first day in Soberton or Meonstoke, both of which have excellent pub accommodation and food. Droxford is between Soberton and Meonstoke: Portchester to The White Lion, Soberton is 12.2 miles whereas Portchester to The Bucks Head, Meonstoke is 14.8 miles.

I have suggested Buriton and Chilgrove for the second and third days, again there is excellent food and accommodation. If you wish to take a slower pace and add an additional day, then there is accommodation at the Sustainability Centre (B&B only), and The White Hart, South Harting (accommodation and food).

This guide would perfectly suit someone who would like to explore the churches but prefers to visit by other means of transport, for example bicycle or car. If travelling by car, short sections of the walks are easily identifiable using the suggested OS maps.

Day 1 St Mary Portchester to St Mary Droxford 12.8 miles

Difficulty moderate – mostly flat in Portchester but a steep climb to the Royal Armoury, with outstanding views across Portsmouth Harbour and The Solent, followed by a gentle downward slope to Wickham and an easy walk along the Meon Valley Trail, passing by Soberton, to Droxford.

Day 2 St Mary Droxford to St Mary Buriton 12.9 miles

The most strenuous day. Continue your easy walk along the Meon Valley Trail, passing by Meonstoke, followed by a steep climb up to Old Winchester Hill. Then follow the Monarch's Way and South Downs Way to Butser Hill before finally descending to Buriton.

Day 3 St Mary Buriton, St Mary South Harting and St Mary North Marden to Chilgrove 10.3 miles

Another steep climb from Buriton up onto the South Downs. Walk along the South Downs Way before descending to South Harting, then returning to the South Downs Way and onto Harting Down, before leaving the South Downs Way to North Marden and Chilgrove.

Day 4 Chilgrove, St Mary Singleton, St Mary East Lavant and the Lady Chapel Chichester Cathedral 10.9 miles

Initially an easy walk on country lanes, then a gentle climb through the West Dean estate before descending into Singleton, followed by a steep climb over The Trundle with magnificent views of Chichester and the Solent beyond before descending to East Lavant and Chichester Cathedral.

Maps

The walking guide maps give an outline of each day's walk. The written guides are detailed. You can download the route in OS maps or GPX from the Mary's Crescent website (**www.maryscrescent.com**). I used the OS Explorer maps (4 cm to 1km, 2.5 in to 1 mile) OL3 and OL8 to explore and define the routes.

Use the suggested OS maps, or visit the website for additional circular walks of 2 to 5 miles from each church and cycle routes between the churches.

You can download the walks from the website:
www.maryscrescent.com

It goes without saying that the Countryside Code should be followed and care taken to check for ticks that may be carrying Lyme disease.

www.gov.uk/government/publications/the-countryside-code/the-countryside-code-advice-for-countryside-visitors

Travel

For those happy to leave their car there is free parking in the streets near Portchester Castle. Portchester railway station is on the main Portsmouth to Southampton line and is a 0.9 mile walk from the Castle. There is a regular and frequent train service from Chichester to Portchester.

Church Opening Times

The churches on this route are open from 10am to 4pm.

St Mary North Marden is permanently open.

Chichester Cathedral is open on weekdays and Saturday 9am–5pm, on Sunday 12 midday–2pm. Choral evensong is at 3pm on Sunday and 5.30pm on all other days.

Accommodation and Food:

Portchester – there is no accommodation in Portchester, the nearest hotels are in Port Solent and Portsmouth.

Portsmouth – The Marriott **https://www.marriott.com/en-us/ hotels/pmeha-portsmouth-marriott-hotel/overview/**

Port Solent – Premier Inn **https://www.premierinn.com/gb/en/ hotels/england/hampshire/portsmouth/portsmouth-port-solent.html**

Wickham – near the Meon Valley Trail, Woodlands Cottage Farm provides B&B accommodation: **https://woodlands-cottage.inn. fan/**

Soberton – The White Lion **www.thewhitelionsoberton.com**

Meonstoke – The Bucks Head **www.thebucksheadmeonstoke.co.uk**

Sustainability Centre – Leydene Park **www.sustainability-centre.org**

Buriton – Five Bells Pub **www.fivebells-buriton.co.uk**

Nest Hotel and Restaurant **www.thenesthotelburiton.co.uk**

South Harting – The White Hart **www.the-whitehart.co.uk**

Chilgrove – The White Horse **www.thewhitehorse.co.uk**

Chichester – there is a wealth of places to stay and eat in Chichester, your best option is to use your search engine to find something suitable.

Food only:

Cormorant pub, Portchester: **www.cormorantpub.co.uk**
Portchester – St Mary's Tearoom **https://www.stmary-portchester. org.uk/tea-room/**
Portsdown Hill – Royal Armoury **https://royalarmouries.org/venue/ fort-nelson/**
Wickham – numerous pubs and cafés
Droxford – Bakers Arms **https://www.thebakersarmsdroxford.com/**
Wilfrids Café, in St Mary's church, Droxford **www.wilfrids.org**
Sustainability Centre – Beech Café **www.thebeechcafe.co.uk**
QE Country Park Centre **www.hants.gov.uk/thingstodo/ countryparks/qecp**
South Harting – The White Hart **www.the-whitehart.co.uk**
Singleton – The Partridge Inn **www.thepartridgeinn.co.uk**
East Lavant – The Royal Oak **www.royaloakeastlavant.co.uk**
Chichester has numerous cafés and restaurants

FOUR-DAY WALKS IN DETAIL

Day 1: St Mary Portchester to St Mary Droxford 12.8 miles

The walk takes you beside Portsmouth harbour and through the urban housing of Portchester before climbing Portsdown hill and through the countryside of southern Hampshire to Wickham and the Meon Valley Trail to Droxford. High tide covers two small areas of the harbourside walk. Please check tide times and, if necessary, follow the guide instruction to avoid them.

You could spend a whole day visiting the royal castle of Portchester and the Priory church of St Mary.

Park in the Castle parking area (fee paying) or local side streets (free).

Portchester Castle

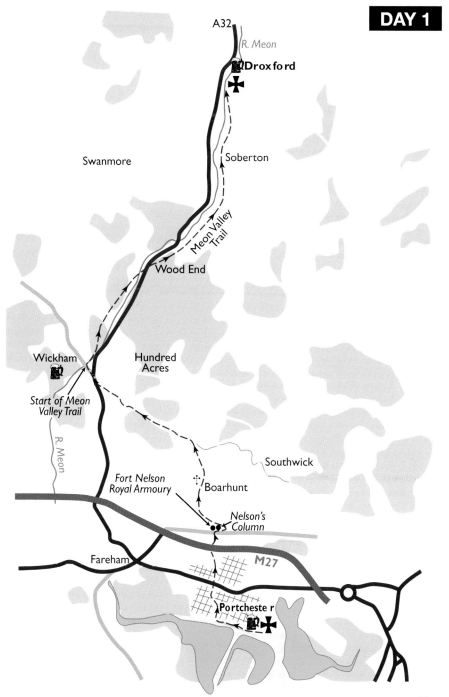

DAY 1

A32

R. Meon

Droxford

Swanmore

Soberton

Meon Valley Trail

Wood End

Wickham

Hundred Acres

Start of Meon Valley Trail

R. Meon

Southwick

Fort Nelson Royal Armoury

Boarhunt

Nelson's Column

Fareham

M27

Portchester

Castle wall with gardrobe (toilet) chutes from Augustinian priory

You approach the castle on foot from Portchester railway station.

The outer castle walls and outer bailey are open every day. St Mary's church is in the outer bailey within the outer castle walls. The inner castle walls and keep are managed by English Heritage and opening times vary:

www.english-heritage.org.uk/visit/places/portchester-castle

Originally a Roman fortress and one of the chain of "Saxon Shore Forts" it was built about the time of Constantine the Great at the end of the 3rd century. The solid walls were still standing in medieval times and were refurbished during Henry I's reign to make the outer bailey of a new castle. The north-west corner was completely refurbished into the inner bailey and keep that you can see today. It would have been an impressive and daunting sight when approached by foot during Henry's reign.

St Mary within Portchester Castle

Priory church of St Mary

The south-east quarter of the roman fortress formed the precinct of an Augustinian priory founded in about 1128 although there would likely have been an earlier church. It continued to serve as a local parish church after the priors moved to Southwick, only a few years following its dedication, in about 1150.

It would continue to have an important role in the lives of the Plantagenet kings, both for ceremony and religious services, because the castle became a major embarkation point for campaigns in France led by English kings.

It is one of the finest Romanesque churches in Wessex, faced in fine ashlar stone – like the castle – both inside and out.

The present-day layout differs from medieval times, when there were both north and south transepts, a longer chancel and a north chapel. The dilapidated south transept was demolished in 1577, as well as the north chapel and part of the east end of the chancel.

Inside it has an austere, simple and impressive feel with little to indicate its original dedication. What would have been present over 500 years ago has been demolished and whitewashed over.

43

St Mary Portchester

West Door ❶

Font ❷

Arcaded Recesses ❸

What to look for:

1. You approach through the wonderful west door's stone columns and arches with intricate Norman carving, to enter the impressive tall long Nave. ❶

2. On your right in the south wall, almost immediately, is a doorway to what would have been the cloister but now leads into the St Mary's Tearoom: open daily 10am-4pm.

3. Opposite, on your left along the north wall, is the font – it is ancient and contemporary with the priory, finely carved and made of Caen stone with wonderful intersecting vine leaves including men with other fauna and flora. ❷

4. Further along the north wall there is a blocked up entrance believed to have been used for royal processions and possibly religious ceremonies too.

5. Continuing along the north wall is a low side window, possibly used for hearing confessions or giving alms, or for those outside the church to observe the moment of transubstantiation – when the host was raised by the priest.

6. The north transept has arcaded recesses – seating for the priors during Mass. ❸

7. There are enormous but elegant tower arches, and you can clearly see where the south transept was demolished, a wall now forming what would have been the entrance. There are filled-in holes in the north and south walls close to the chancel archway suggesting fixings for a rood loft and screen, although no information of its history exists.

8. The chancel is a shadow of its former self; the roof is much lower than that of the nave and south transept, and was lowered in the 16th century (the original height can be judged by looking from the outside of the church at the east end of the tower). Remnants of arcading along the walls can be seen; originally the chancel was longer with no doubt an apsidal or semi-circular end. Perhaps when partially demolished a piscina and aumbry were removed.

Exit Portchester Castle by the southern (seaward) gate and look over towards Portsmouth Naval dockyard, harbour and the Spinnaker tower.

As a memorial to the journey about to be taken I picked up a cockle shell from the beach and carried it with me to the shingle garden in the cathedral cloister.

Turn right along the coastal path, notice the garderobe chutes from the Augustinian Priory when its west transept and Priory accommodation was attached to the castle perimeter wall.

Your route is westward along the harbour wall for 1.2 miles until you reach Wicor Mill Lane, where you turn inland.

If it is high tide and the water is touching the embankment you won't be able to take the shore route, instead continue around the castle wall to the road and walk down towards the Cormorant pub. Take the left turn into Hospital Lane and continue until you reach the sea, turn right and continue along the sea wall.

If the tide does not touch the embankment and there is visible beach, you can continue along the coastal path.

The path goes along the edge of the beach on the harbour wall and is clearly marked.

In two places, for 25 metres, the path lowers to beach level beside the breeze block walls of gardens.

After the second breeze block garden wall you continue along the coastal path, there are open grass areas to your right with a play park. You continue on the coastal path until ahead you will see some fairly new housing and on one roofline there are obvious solar panels. On your left there is an outfall pipe running onto the beach. Soon after this and before you reach the new houses, turn right into Wicor Mill Lane.

Go to the end of Wicor Mill Lane and turn left into White Hart Lane which, after a short distance, curves round to the right to become Cornaway Lane. Cornaway Lane ends in a busy roundabout, take the pedestrian underpass on your left and emerge onto Dore Avenue, which is directly across the roundabout opposite Cornaway Lane.

The road goes uphill forming a railway bridge, and you will see Portchester Crematorium on your left. Turn into Upper Cornaway Lane, and keeping the crematorium on your left, keep going until you see a large sign "Northfield Park", your footpath is just to the right of this.

The path goes gently uphill. Turn right at the end of the path and immediately left onto a footbridge across the M27. Before crossing the bridge look back over Portsmouth harbour with the Isle of Wight in the distance.

At the end of the footbridge turn right and continue uphill until you come out onto a green pasture where there is a sign saying "Fort Nelson Nature Reserve", turn left and keep going uphill along the marked path.

The path comes out on a busy road opposite the entrance to Fort Nelson (which is now the Royal Armouries Museum and open to the public), cross the road and turn right up steps following the sign for pedestrians.

> The Royal Armoury is housed in one of "Palmerston's Follies" – a huge Victorian brick fort – and is well worth visiting but requires half a day to do it justice:
> **https://royalarmouries.org/venue/fort-nelson/**
> Fort Nelson is one of five Portsdown Forts, built as a result of the 1859 Royal Commission by Lord Palmerston to prevent a French land attack, on the Portsmouth dockyard only 5 miles away, because the older Hilsea Lines at the bottom of the ridge were considered insufficient.

The Royal Armoury – Fort Nelson

47

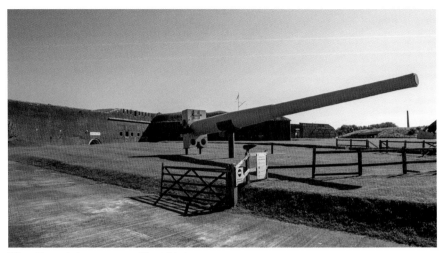

The Royal Armoury – Fort Nelson

Walk past the public entrance to the Royal Armoury (entry is free and you can stop for refreshments at the café). Continue into the public car park and ahead you will see a tall stone column which was "consecrated to the memory of Lord Viscount Nelson". It's certainly worth walking round and admiring the view:
http://www.memorialsinportsmouth.co.uk/portsmouth-north/ nelson-column.htm
Go past the column through a small gate and turn left onto a minor road, then left again after a few metres and through another gate and you are now on an open grassy area with Fort Nelson car park on your left and a mound on your right.

Bear left and through a metal gate, Fort Nelson is on your left, notice the deep moat and gun embrasures – look right across the valley and you will see the South Downs in the distance.

You cross a stile and the path veers to the right across a field ending at a small tarmacked lane, between the house and pylon you see across the field. There is a fingerpost indicating Allan King's Way and you turn right.

The road joins another much more busy country road and you turn right downhill. Walk carefully along the road, facing the traffic for a short distance until you can cross the road and go through the churchyard gate

Nelson's Column

of the simple two cell Anglo-Saxon church dedicated to St Nicholas.

I made an exception with this church as it is directly on the route and it seemed churlish to ignore it because it is not dedicated to the Virgin Mary.

Leave the church behind you and walk down the road, Manor Farm and pond are across the road on your right.

After 50 yards on your left you will see two metal gates into farmland, take the second gate which has an HCC medallion saying, "Allan King's Way".

49

The church is wholly owned and administered by the Southwick Estate under the care of the Squire, Mr Thistlethwayte; it is a Donative Lay Peculiar. 'Donative' describes the legal ability of the owner, to gift or will property, in this case a church. 'Peculiar' is the state of a church exempt from the jurisdiction of the Ordinary (the Bishop), in whose Diocese the churches are. The term 'Lay' is used to distinguish the fact that a church is not 'Royal'. The Squire acts as a 'Lay Bishop' with the intrinsic authority to appoint a Vicar/Chaplain, a Verger and a Church Warden.

It is infrequently open but inside there are several reminders of its medieval past: piscina, aumbry, Saxon font, medieval scroll decoration around the blocked north door and medieval stone image brackets beside the altar.

If you are only able to walk around the outside, note the blocked medieval and Saxon entrances in the nave and a very small priest's entrance into the chancel.

Continue along a well-made-up farm track which ends at a field. On your right there is an HCC sign indicating the path keeps to the right-hand side of the field.

St Nicholas Church, South Boarhunt

You come to another HCC sign and see a bridge crossing a stream, follow this into the next field. Turn left and head towards the wooden gate you can see across the field.

Go through the gate and over the two footbridges and ahead is a path between two horse paddocks with post/rail fencing.

You see Bere Farm ahead and when you reach it turn right and then left after 200 metres signposted to Bere Farmhouse. There is a good farm track which is initially straight before bearing right, at which point you carry straight along the clearly marked footpath across fields.

The path takes you through a hedge, a signpost indicates your way straight ahead. The path eventually widens leading onto a minor road.

Turn right and then almost immediately left onto another good track that takes you all the way to the busy A32. Cross the road (be careful!) and turn right towards Wickham village along the pavement. As you approach the roundabout ahead, your path bears left towards Wickham village. Keep on the pavement and you will see a railway bridge ahead of you, cross the road.

If you want to stop in Wickham, continue under the bridge and the village square is on your right. There are a number of eating and resting places in the village centre which is a wide well-proportioned historic conservation area. It was built around the ford crossing over the river Meon for the Roman road from Chichester to Winchester.

If not, take the incline up to the disused railway track and turn right onto the public path which goes all the way to Droxford.

You are now on the **Meon Valley Trail**:
www.hants.gov.uk/thingstodo/countryside/finder/meonvalleytrail
You walk along the trail for 4.15 miles until you reach Soberton village. The trail follows the line of the old railway from Alton to Gosport, a victim of government minister Richard Beeching's report "The Reshaping of British Railways" in 1963. It is a gentle level walk with lovely views of woodland and the meandering river Meon.

You pass under six bridges, in a deep cut the seventh bridge is made of iron and has a large metal pipe running parallel to the bridge. At this point you leave the Meon Valley Trail.

You can take the steep path to the right in front of the bridge but the easier path is 100 metres beyond the bridge on your right.

Bridge across Meon Valley Trail at Soberton

If you are staying at the White Lion pub (**www.thewhitelionsoberton. com**) in Soberton turn uphill towards the church and follow the lane. Directly across the village green is the pub.

If not, turn downhill on the tarmac lane back across the bridge and a little way further on the right follow the Wayfarer's Walk signs. This is a delightful route across meadows and leads down beside the River Meon to Droxford.

River Meon

The White Lion, Soberton

(If the weather is poor or wet underfoot stick to the railway and continue to the next bridge. After 50 metres, on the left before the bridge, there is an old siding with signs explaining how the railway line was used during World War II. You will see there is an incline which takes you up to the path on the bridge.)

Cross the two footbridges over the River Meon and you will see Droxford Church ahead of you.

Visit St Mary and All Saints Church which is open from 10am to 4pm.

Walk to the left of the church and out onto the main street past the Village Hall. Turn right for the Bakers Arms.

St Mary and All Saints Droxford

As you approach this classic Norman church try and imagine the original building; no porch, aisles or tower. The main nave and chancel were built in the 12th century; the aisles were later additions – the north in the 13th century and the south in the 14th century, when presumably the impressive Norman entrance archway was also repositioned. The tower, the upper windowed section of the chancel (clerestory) and steep nave roof in the Sussex "catslide" manner are all post-Reformation.

St Mary Droxford

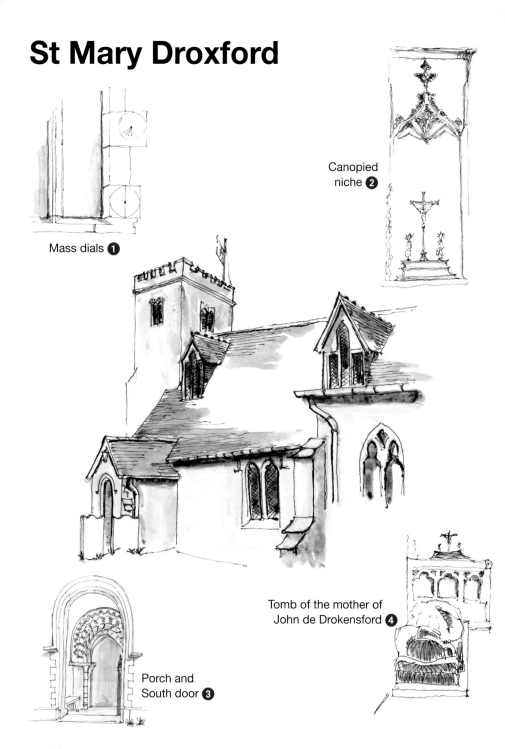

Canopied
niche ❷

Mass dials ❶

Tomb of the mother of
John de Drokensford ❹

Porch and
South door ❸

What to look for:

1. Mass dials. Within the porch is the carved Norman archway, if you look closely at the jambs on either side of the door you will find medieval Mass dials. Today the dials clearly receive no sun, however in the 12th century when the doorway went straight into the nave, before the south aisle or porch were added, they would have usefully indicated when church services were due. There are two further dials outside, on the east jamb of the window of the south-east chapel, one above the other. ❶ ❸

2. The massive interior columns were created from the original nave walls when the aisles were added.

3. Rood stair opening high up on the left of the Norman chancel arch – it must have opened out to a rood loft incorporating a massive wooden rood beam with the Rood and figures of Saints Mary and John either side. Probably a tympanum made of wood and painted would have filled the space of the chancel arch behind the rood loft and beam; an arresting spiritual dynamic between heaven – the chancel – and earth – the nave.

4. North chapel, now Wilfrid's Café – a community café (www.wilfrids.org) where drinks and light refreshments are served (check opening times on the website). Sitting at one of the tables gives you a unique opportunity to observe the piscina, aumbry and remains of the lower opening to the rood loft stair. There is also some faint evidence of medieval wall painting on the chapel's east wall.

5. South chapel, where restoration in 1903 revealed a fine canopied niche in the east wall, which had suffered Puritan desecration; the niche is likely to have contained a statue to the Virgin Mary. The chapel also contains a piscina and the Purbeck marble stone tomb effigy of probably the mother of John de Drokensford, who died in 1329. John was chancellor to Edward II and later Bishop of Bath and Wells. The tomb effigy was found in a nearby field in 1820, no doubt discarded during the Reformation upheaval. ❷ ❹

6. Graffiti – Hexafoil or Daisy wheel: on the north-east chamfered corner of the pillar opposite and left of the south door (porch) entrance.

Day 2: St Mary Droxford to St Mary Buriton 12.9 miles

Your second day takes you back onto the Meon Valley Trail and then onto the South Downs Way, across Old Winchester Hill to Leydene Park and Butser Hill before descending to Queen Elizabeth Country park and finally Buriton.

Trace your steps back to the church and walk through the churchyard. With the church behind you, at the left-hand corner of the churchyard you will find a gate leading into a field. Go through and turn left and walk to the end of the field where ahead you'll see the Mill House.

Take the marked public path to the right of the Mill House entrance, cross the footbridge over the mill race and along a tarmacked path, to cross another footbridge over the Meon River. Keep going along the quiet lane ahead and on your right after 300 metres you will see a path going uphill towards the old railway another 300 metres away. Take this path, it is initially straight but then winds through woodland, and follow it all the way onto the old railway. You are now back on the Meon Valley Trail (MVT). Turn left towards West Meon.

As the path bends round to the right you will see the old railway platform for Droxford Station **(https://en.wikipedia.org/wiki/Droxford_railway_station)**.

In 1944, amid World War II, Droxford station was used by the Prime Minister Winston Churchill as his base during preparations for the Normandy landings. Based in an armoured train parked in the sidings at Droxford, Churchill met with numerous ministers, military commanders and leaders of allied nations on 4 June 1944, shortly before the landings were due to take place.

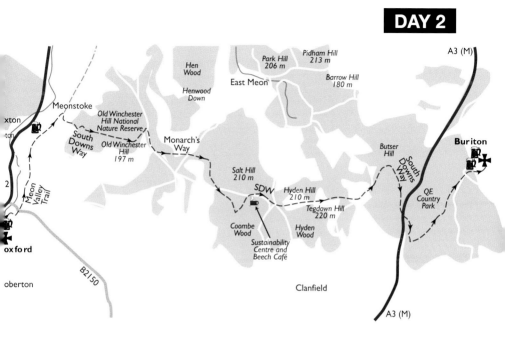

The path then bends to the left and you cross the B2150 via the railway bridge.

Keep on the MVT, after ¾ mile you pass under a bridge. You are now passing nearby Meonstoke.

If you are staying at the Bucks Head:

(**https://www.thebucksheadmeonstoke.co.uk/**) take the left turning shortly after the bridge into Meonstoke village.

You follow the road down into the village and turn right gently uphill past pretty 17th- and 18th-century cottages and houses, then turn left at the top going downhill to the Bucks Head on your right. To return to the MVT turn left uphill out of the Bucks Head and at the summit continue on the road first left and then right where it becomes Pound Lane. 100m ahead on the left, just before the road bridge, there are steps down to rejoin the MVT.

If not staying at the Bucks Head:

Continue along the MVT under one further bridge. The next bridge ahead has been dismantled and you must come off here. The road beneath the bridge tends to flood in wet weather and you will see an alternative "permissive path avoiding flood" ahead of you, which provides steps off the railway embankment on your left-hand side, avoiding the worst flooded area. You walk across Stocks Lane and get back onto the old railway / Meon Valley Trail.

There are lovely views on both sides, especially to your right where you will see Old Winchester Hill dominating the landscape and where your journey takes you.

After a further $2/3$ mile there are signs for the South Downs Way, first on the left marked to Exton – which you do not take – and then on the right which you do take.

As you come down off the Meon Valley Trail there is a small footbridge crossing a ditch; you are now on the South Downs Way National Trail heading eastwards.

Old Winchester Hill from the Meon Valley Trail

Old Winchester Hill National Nature Reserve

You continue uphill on a well-made hardcore path. You come to a fingerpost which marks the Monarch's Way downhill and to your left, but you keep straight on uphill where both Monarch's Way and SDW run parallel on either side of a hedge.

After 200 metres the paths diverge, the SDW veers to the right, but you continue straight uphill on the Monarch's Way and after 100 metres go through a metal gate to enter **Old Winchester Hill National Nature Reserve**. **https://en.wikipedia.org/wiki/Old_Winchester_Hill**

Continue uphill going through the Iron Age fort western gateway to the summit where there is a trig point and panorama plaque between two tumuli. On a clear day there are fantastic views southwards to the Solent and Isle of Wight.

After taking in the panorama continue walking and leave the fort by its eastern gateway, turn left downhill for a few metres before passing through the gate on your right, where the SDW rejoins your path once again.

The Solent from Old Winchester Hill

There is once more a hardcore path, continue along this for 300 metres and ahead of you is the nature reserve entrance and a metal gate off Old Winchester Hill Lane.

Exit via the metal gate and turn right along Old Winchester Hill Lane, you are now on the Monarch's Way. It's a busy road so take care! You follow the road for 600m and at the signpost on your left, cross over a stile and then almost immediately cross a fence into the wood on your right.

Take the marked path downhill through the wood, it emerges at a stile over a steep escarpment. Follow the path downhill; straight ahead across the valley you can see the two aerials on Wether Down and to your left over Whitewool Farm is Hen Wood. Follow the path across the field which takes you onto a small lane where you turn left and very soon turn right into a field which skirts the foot of Chidden Down keeping to the Monarch's Way.

This path leads to another narrow metalled lane, turn right uphill and continue to the summit where you re-join Old Winchester Hill Lane.

Paragliders near Old Winchester Hill

Straight across Old Winchester Hill Lane are two marked footpaths, avoid the right-hand path (Monarch's Way) and take the left-hand path which bears slightly left.

Continue along the path, there are wonderful views southwards; on a clear day you can easily make out the silhouetted ship shape of the defence research establishment (Dstl) sited on top of Portsdown Hill above Portsmouth, and further west the outline of Fort Nelson – home to the Royal Armoury which you passed on the Portchester to Droxford section.

The path leads onto a narrow metalled road, continue along the road for 300 metres, until on your left just before an oak wood, there is a footpath bearing north, follow this footpath with the wood on your right and it takes you back onto Old Winchester Hill Lane.

Turn right, you are now back on the SDW and almost immediately on your right is the newly refurbished Eco Lodge – part of The Sustainability

View across to East Meon

Centre, a charitable learning and study centre for sustainability – part of the Leydene Estate:
https://www.sustainability-centre.org/accommodation.html

The Eco Lodge offers B&B, group bookings, Yurts and self-catering accommodation.

You can purchase refreshments from the Beech Café in the Sustainability Centre which is a little further on your right-hand side (check opening times: open Thursday-Sunday when I visited for an excellent coffee and vegetarian sandwich).

From the Sustainability Centre, you continue along the path by the roadside, which leaves the road to hug the boundary of Leydene Park, before rejoining the road at a crossroads.

Leydene Estate was created in 1913 by William Peel, grandson of Sir Robert Peel the Victorian Prime Minister. The house was taken over by the Royal Navy during World War II – named HMS *Mercury* – and finally it was sold for housing in the 1990s: **https://www.eastmeonhistory.org.uk/content/catalogue_item/ leydene-house**

Go straight across and after 150 metres you cross a further road (Clanfield to East Meon) onto a SDW marked track. Continue along the made-up track with Hyden wood on your right and open countryside to East Meon on your left.

The track gently rises uphill and levels off, before gently going downhill. You pass farm buildings and a house on your right and the track becomes metalled, finally joining Hogs Lodge Lane, where you turn left. The lane slopes gently up to Butser Hill where you can see an aerial straight ahead.

On your right there are wonderful views to the south over to the Isle of Wight, Chichester Harbour and the Solent.

At the end of the lane, on the left, you find a sign welcoming you to Queen Elizabeth Country Park:
https://www.hants.gov.uk/thingstodo/countryparks/qecp

Butser Hill, Queen Elizabeth Country Park

Next to it there is a fingerpost marked SDW directing you to turn half right. Take this path which skirts below Butser Hill aerial and car park, through a gate where a SDW fingerpost directs you to turn right gently downhill. Continue downhill, once again with wonderful views marred now by the site and traffic noise from the A3.

The path levels out and you pass through a gate. The path turns left through a hedge and on the other side there is a fingerpost on your left indicating SDW is straight on. You cross a metalled road and take the path running alongside to go via the underpass beneath the A3. As you exit the underpass, on your left, you will see a newly constructed slope bearing your path, take this and go straight ahead into the woods and immediately you will see a fingerpost marking the SDW.

The path goes gently uphill, below you on your right is the Queen Elizabeth Country Park information centre and car park (refreshments are available). The path levels out and then goes gently downhill, at the bottom a SDW sign guides you left and then straight across a metalled road where there is another SDW fingerpost. You go uphill for 200 metres and a SDW fingerpost directs you left. Continue uphill following the SDW signs, eventually the path flattens out and then goes gently downhill to merge with a larger made-up path coming in from the right. Keep on this path going uphill, don't be tempted to take any path leading off to your left or right. After 300 metres it begins to descend, you will find a bench on your right with a small stone statue – a sheep on a square plinth – which pays tribute to the hundreds of years of downland sheep the environment has supported.

The path continues to descend and in due course you will come to a public car park. Go straight through. The SDW turns right but straight ahead of you follow the fingerpost marking Shipwrights Way and Hangers Way, at the entrance to Buriton Chalk Pits nature reserve.

The chalk pits were active prior to World War II. Chalk was heated in kilns to make lime, used for building purposes:
https://learning.southdowns.gov.uk/wp-content/uploads/ sites/2/2015/08/Buriton-Chalk-Pit-Industrial-Nature-Trail.pdf

The hardcore path runs downhill, steeply at times, and then through a tunnel beneath the main London to Portsmouth railway. You exit onto

St Mary's, Buriton

a metalled path which passes two limestone and brick cottages on your right before finally ending by the village pond.

St Mary's is across the pond to your right.

If you are staying at The Five Bells or The Nest Hotel, turn left and both are nearby on the right.

www.fivebells-buriton.co.uk/
www.thenesthotelburiton.co.uk/

St Mary the Virgin Buriton

The church – both nave and chancel – that you see today were built between 1150 and 1200 although a church is also listed in the Domesday Book of 1086 and may well have been Saxon originally.

The original tower was destroyed by fire, following a lightning strike in 1712.

My initial impression is of a church burdened by monuments to local Victorian families faded to reveal sensitive reminders of its dedication and medieval past.

65

St Mary Buriton

South door

Piscina and three-step sedilia ❶

Virgin and Child ❷

Font ❸

What to look for:

1. Graffiti: As you enter the church look to your right. On the doorway to the tower are carved VV (Virgin of Virgins) and nearby M (Mary). There are bore holes in the shape of a Cross, created to produce stone dust to add potency to medieval remedies. Look carefully at the third south pillar from the west, on its eastern side are three interlocking circles 14cm in diameter faintly inscribed – thought to trap malign forces.

2. The striking Norman round arches of the nave have pillars with plain, scalloped and foliated capitals built circa 1180. The arches were formed by the original addition of south and north aisles. The south aisle was rebuilt in the 13th century and the north aisle was rebuilt in 1780.

3. The right-hand window of a pair at the east end of the north aisle, inspired by Burne-Jones, shows St Gabriel holding a lily to Mary at the annunciation.

4. The chancel screen is a Victorian copy of a 16th-century screen.

5. The finely proportioned east window is in the English Decorated style from 1280. Carved heads adorn the outer supports – on the left a bishop, on the right a king.

6. There is a beautifully executed three step sedilia in the south wall of the chancel, with trefoil arch and separating stone panels. The piscina to the left has the same trefoil arch design. On the opposite wall, to the right of the vestry door, is an aumbry. ❶

7. The window in the south wall of the chancel deserves a close inspection; the left-hand section of the lowest portion is blocked off and it is thought that the right-hand section, now glazed, originally had wooden shutters inside and out, possibly acting as a confessional for use by travelling friars - known as a 'low side window'. On the left-hand window jamb are faint traces of a medieval wall painting of the Virgin and Child. The right-hand jamb has traces of painted scroll work. ❷

8. Whilst you are in the chancel, look at the floor beneath the choir stalls nearest to the altar, where there are three medieval encaustic tiles on the right and left side, and more beneath the stalls. They are identical to tiles found at Durford Abbey dating from 1260.

9. The font is 12th-century, square with cylindrical supporting shafts. There is clear evidence of damage to the bowl where religious symbols have been chiselled off leaving a rough discoloured surface. ❸

10. There is a very formal east window in the south aisle depicting the risen Christ flanked by Saints Mary and John. Further west along the south aisle wall is a millennium window depicting Mary directing the child Christ – whose feet are in immersed in "living water" streaming from the South Downs. A lovely symbol of the Buriton parishioners' faith.

Day 3 St Mary Buriton to Chilgrove
10.3 miles

Today's walk takes you back up to the South Downs Way (SDW). You follow the SDW as far as South Harting, where you descend to the village and visit the church of St Mary and St Gabriel. You climb back to the SDW and continue to Harting Down, where you leave the SDW to visit St Mary, North Marden before finally arriving at Chilgrove.

With St Mary's church behind you, turn left, walk through the car park, ahead and slightly to the left is a gate with a fingerpost pointing in two directions. Turn left and walk parallel to the South Downs, between a shallow ditch on your left and a field on your right. Follow this path until you come to a gate. Pass through and turn right uphill along the winding farm track, at first gently then more steeply between banks thick in springtime with wild garlic, until it flattens out before joining the SDW.

Turn left onto the SDW which is a narrow tarmacked lane with wonderful views, especially following thinning of the ash trees due to ash dieback. When the narrow lane joins a wider lane, turn left as directed to continue on the SDW. You see Sunwood Farm on the road below and ahead of you.

At Sunwood Farm the lane turns sharply left. Soon after, you take a stony track on your right, signposted SDW. It rises gently ahead of you and when you reach the summit there are marvellous long views to the

Vandalian Tower: Built in 1774 by Sir Matthew Fetherstonhaugh of Uppark (now owned by the National Trust **www.nationaltrust**) to commemorate the founding of the short-lived British colony of Vandalia established in America.

DAY 3

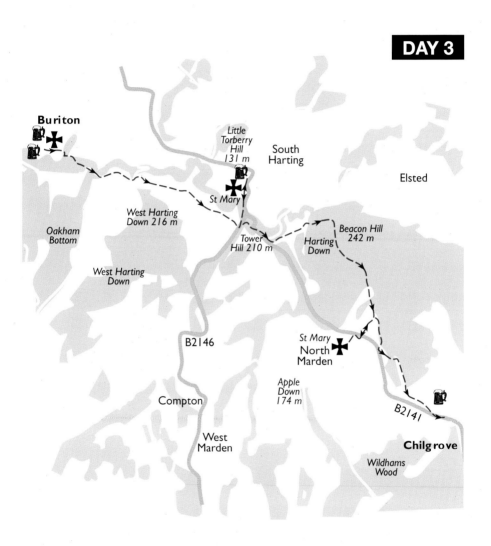

Buriton

Little
Torberry
Hill
131 m

South
Harting

Elsted

West Harting
Down 216 m

St Mary

Oakham
Bottom

Tower
Hill 210 m

Harting
Down

Beacon Hill
242 m

West Harting
Down

B2146

St Mary
North
Marden

Apple
Down
174 m

Compton

B2141

West
Marden

Chilgrove

Wildhams
Wood

View northward from South Downs Way

left. The path then descends before rising again and crossing a metalled lane onto a track known as Forty Acre Lane.

As you initially descend you can see ahead, on a crest of the South Downs known as Tower Hill, the ruined Vandalian Tower.

On your left, just before the path joins the B2146, there is a fingerpost beside a metal barrier. Turn left downhill to South Harting. Just below is a new deer fence enclosure protecting recently planted trees replacing the felled ash. Pass through the gate into the enclosure and follow the path downhill, exit the enclosure and continue downhill passing a small area of water on your left which was the reservoir from where water was pumped to Uppark House. Indeed the house would not have been sited high up on the downs unless one of the owner's forbears, Sir Edward Ford, had not invented the first pump capable of lifting water a considerable height. You enter a recreation area with children's play park and are now in the outskirts of South Harting.

As the path flattens out it passes through a car park and leads

Vandalian Tower

onto the B2146. Turn left and take care! There is no pavement so you must walk 150m on the road before coming across the church of St Mary and St Gabriel on your left.

St Mary and St Gabriel South Harting

The church is large and cruciform and was badly damaged by fire in 1576. The subsequent rebuilding has made it difficult to ascertain with certainty how old the church is.

What you see is mostly 14th-century but there are signs of earlier work, for example the remarkably tall nave with narrow walls is thought to be 11th-century or even earlier, possibly Saxon. The chancel is less wide than the nave, the core of which is 13th-century. It is thought that the tower, transepts and aisles are all 14th-century. The east arch of the crossing tower is quite elaborate and has an order of dogtooth stonework.

St Mary South Harting

Font **2**

Rood loft piscina **1**

Clock stair **3**

What to look for:

1. Crane your neck upwards, high on the south side of the east crossing arch is a trefoil-headed piscina; it must have been for a rood loft altar, and is all that now remains of the rood and rood loft. ❶

2. In 1610 a chapel was added on the north side, dedicated to the Caryll family, but this subsequently fell into disrepair and was demolished. The Caryll effigy along with the Cowper family effigies now stand in the North Transept.

3. The font is 13th-century, the bowl is incised with trefoil arcading and is of Purbeck marble; the four shafts and base are 19th-century. ❷

4. There are some fine statues – a simple, contemplative Madonna and Child by Karin Jonzen that was commissioned to replace an ancient Spanish 14th-century wooden statue, stolen in 1985. In the south transept there is also a dramatic life-size St Gabriel by Philip Jackson poised in flight – I was struck by the statue representation of the messenger (Gabriel) being greater than the message (Mary).

5. In the chancel is a very worn fragment of 13th-century stone showing a head and shoulders.

6. There is a charming stained-glass window of the Madonna and Child in the south aisle.

7. There is some wonderful (post-Reformation) woodwork; look at the roof of the chancel rebuilt after the fire in 1577, and a stunning wooden staircase to the bell tower, paid for by Lady Fetherstonhaugh from nearby Uppark and made by her estate carpenter in 1853. Apparently it was to ease the job of the clock winder who had to climb a wooden ladder on a daily basis to wind the clock. ❸

8. The distinctive copper spire which can be seen for miles around was rebuilt in 1935 following storm damage.

9. Outside do have a look at the elegant and simple stone war memorial by well-known sculptor Eric Gill.

A little further down on the left is the White Hart pub. It's a great pub with good food and accommodation.

After exploring the church and possibly taking refreshment, you return the way you came back to the SDW.

When you reach the SDW turn left and cross the road. Continue on the SDW, which gently rises and passes through delightful beech woodland. The Vandalian Tower is on your right, above you and out of sight from the path. Continue on this path until you cross the road once more to enter Harting Down, owned by the National Trust.

Ahead you will see a thick hedgerow and the NT car park on the right, take the path that goes to the right of the hedgerow – the SDW goes to the left of the hedge but there is a much better walking path running parallel to the SDW but 25m to its right. You climb to the summit of Harting Down with extensive views leftwards. Below you

South Harting village from Harting Down

will see the spire of St Mary's. If you are walking in the spring you are very likely to see wild orchids in the grassy meadows and nearby copse.

Continue on this path uphill, down the other side and up again where the path turns left through the thick hedge. After a few paces downhill pass through a gate, continue downhill to the bottom where there is another gate and on your left a fingerpost mounted on a flint plinth. This marks the SDW where you take a right turn to go gently uphill.

You could take a more vigorous route straight uphill onto Beacon Hill where, from the trig point, there are amazing views of the countryside over to the Solent and Isle of Wight. At the trig point you bear south towards the sea, crossing the swathe of grassland; you keep going until you reach a wooden gate at the point where the SDW takes a left turn. Pass through the gate.

If you chose the more gentle route it takes you up the side of Beacon Hill and on reaching the summit the SDW turns left just before the wooden gate (see previous paragraph). You go through the gate and onto the driveway of Telegraph House, which is hidden behind trees and hedges on the right-hand side.

The driveway to Telegraph House has a wonderful copper beech avenue which is initially straight but then curves to the right. You leave the drive keeping straight on and pass through a small gate onto a "public bridleway". After 100m the path is joined by a farm track coming up from the left, you continue on the track for a further 300m where there is a fingerpost on your right – the main path continues straight on – but you turn right on the "public footpath".

This path runs between ancient hedgerows for 450m before joining the B2141 again where you go straight across and take the path by the fingerpost. You are now in North Marden. Shortly the path bears right, joining a road. You follow the road straight ahead, passing a red letter

Telegraph House is the site of a Semaphore Station built in 1822, which enabled rapid communication between the Admiralty Office London and Portsmouth Naval Base. The current house was built in 1927 by the brother of Bertrand Russell and leased to the philosopher and his wife who ran an unsuccessful "experimental" school from the premises.

Beech Avenue, Telegraph House

box on the left. Just afterwards there is a left turn with a signboard marked "St Mary's Church". Take this turning and keep to your right. The church is tucked away behind trees and hedgerow on the right-hand side.

After visiting the church, retrace your steps across the B2141, and follow the footpath to the main path, where you turn right. Continue along the path until it reaches a metalled road where you turn right uphill.

After a short distance there is a stile on your left with a fingerpost indicating a "public footpath".

Take the path, there are wonderful views of the South Downs across the valley. The path enters a conifer wood and continues initially gently, but then more steeply downhill, traversing the valley side. At the foot of the valley is a metal kissing gate leading onto a meadow. Look across the meadow to your right where there is another metal gate, cross the meadow and pass through. Just ahead, at a four way fingerpost, you turn right on the "public bridleway". 500m further on there is a wooden gate, pass through and join a farm track where you turn right. You pass beneath electricity cables from a nearby pylon and ahead on the left is a fingerpost. Turn left taking the "public footpath" through a kissing gate.

Walk along the valley floor. On the left you pass huge mature beech and oak trees. Pass through the kissing gate ahead of you, straight across the driveway and through a further two kissing gates as the path gradually merges with the B2141. Go through the metal gate at the

The White Horse, Chilgrove

end of the meadow and turn left along the grass verge by the road. Just ahead of you, on the left, is the White Horse pub where excellent food and accommodation are available.

St Mary North Marden

St Mary's was originally a chapel of ease – that is, a subsidiary chapel to St Peter's at East Marden. It is believed to have been founded by Geoffrey son of Azo, who was Sherriff of Hampshire from 1179 to 1189. It figures in the taxation records of Pope Nicholas (1291).

It is a "single cell", which means that the nave and semi-circular apse have no separating chancel arch. It is said to be one of only four in England.

It is charming, peaceful and remote, reminding me of some of the small chapels along the Camino de Santiago. It has no electricity and services are lit by candlelight. Its simple medieval interior is a little spoilt by four wooden panels displaying the Commandments and Lord's Prayer but with no reminders of the church's dedication.

Outside the church, at the west end, is a large wooden bench – it is well worth resting for a few moments to reflect and admire the view across the valley to North Marden Down.

St Mary North Marden

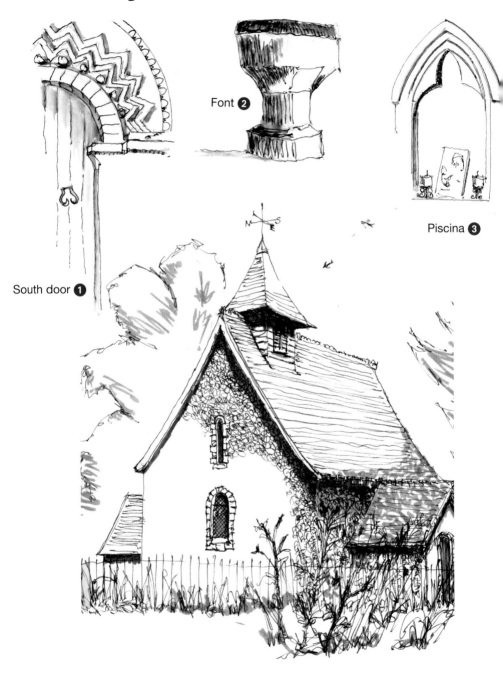

Font ❷

Piscina ❸

South door ❶

What to look for:

1. The church has an elaborate Norman south doorway made of Caen stone with chevrons enclosing a ball shape similar to work at Chichester Cathedral. ❶

2. The font bowl is 12th-century with an octagonal stem added in the 14th century. ❷

3. The three Norman windows in the apse have been restored, but the small window high in the west end is original.

4. There is a trefoil (Latin for three-leaved) 13th-century niche in the apse, probably a piscina although possibly for a statue to the Virgin Mary. ❸

Day 4 Chilgrove to Chichester 10.9 miles

Today's walk starts with a meander along quiet country lanes. You then enter West Dean estate and follow a gentle farm track, which eventually brings you to Singleton and the ancient church of St Mary. You then climb up St Roche's Hill (also known as The Trundle) with lovely views over Chichester Harbour and The Solent, before descending to the church of St Mary, East Lavant and finally the Lady Chapel, Chichester Cathedral.

Leave The White Horse pub at Chilgrove and turn left uphill. After 500m the road bends right, keep going and after a further 400m it bends left and loops round to Staple Ash Farm, where you take the left-hand fork signposted to West Dean. After 250m the road takes a sharp left but you carry straight on taking the farm track – there is a huge limestone rock by the side of the road where your path begins.

Limestone rock

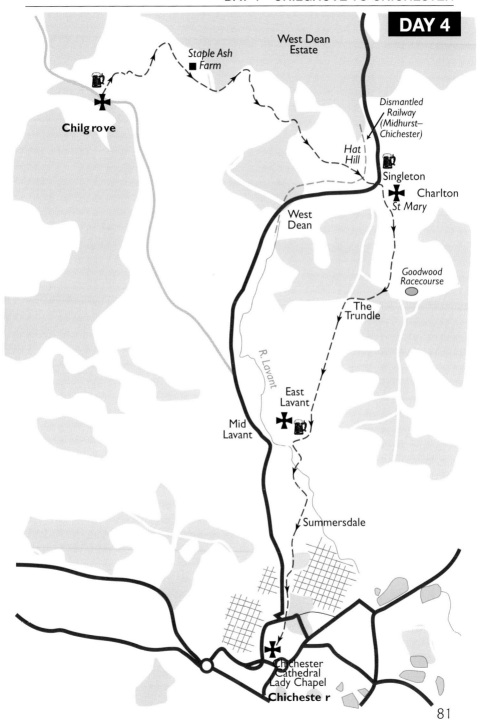

DAY 4

West Dean
Estate

Staple Ash
Farm

Dismantled
Railway
(Midhurst–
Chichester)

Chilgrove

Hat
Hill

Singleton

Charlton

St Mary

West
Dean

Goodwood
Racecourse

The
Trundle

R. Lavant

East
Lavant

Mid
Lavant

Summersdale

Chichester
Cathedral
Lady Chapel

Chichester

West Dean Estate

The farm track goes over a field and ahead you will see a metal kissing gate, pass through and downhill through woodland. At the bottom you re-join the tarmac lane, continue straight ahead and after 100m take the bridleway signpost on your left which skirts West Dean Woods. The track initially has a broken brick surface, made from the rubble generated by the severe bombing of Portsmouth in World War II.

Continue along the track for 750m to a fingerpost and take the right-hand turning to Colworth Barn and cottages. Follow the track downhill and past Colworth Barn, up the other side and through Colworth Farm. A little further on is a pair of flint cottages with hanging tiles on the upper floor. Soon after you turn left at the fingerpost marked "public footpath". After 150m you turn right at the fingerpost and skirt the side of a wood (Drovers NT estate). The path takes a short dog leg to take you to the opposite side of the hedge ahead of you, and you continue straight along this path, passing close by an electricity pylon on your right, crossing a stile and going downhill (which is steep in parts). As you skirt a coppice on your right you see Singleton in the valley below.

Bridge over disused Midhurst to Chichester railway

At the bottom of the hill go down the concrete steps and cross the bridge (which has fine black brick and stone copings) over the disused Midhurst to Chichester railway line. Continue along the path which ends in a stile, cross this and then cross another ahead of you – in

St Mary Singleton

The Blessed Virgin Mary Singleton is mentioned in the Domesday Book. The original church is thought to have been just the tower, with the nave occupying the tower's ground floor and with a small chancel added to the east of the tower.

It may have originally been an Anglo-Saxon minster.

The tower is probably Saxon in origin and the current tall nave was added in the 11th or 12th century. When the current nave was built it is thought to have had an upper floor for priests' accommodation, which was accessed via a triangular-headed opening now visible from within the nave, the high east gable window giving light.

The south aisle and arches were added in the 13th century along with the chancel. The north aisle, arches and porch were added in the 15th century.

St Mary Singleton

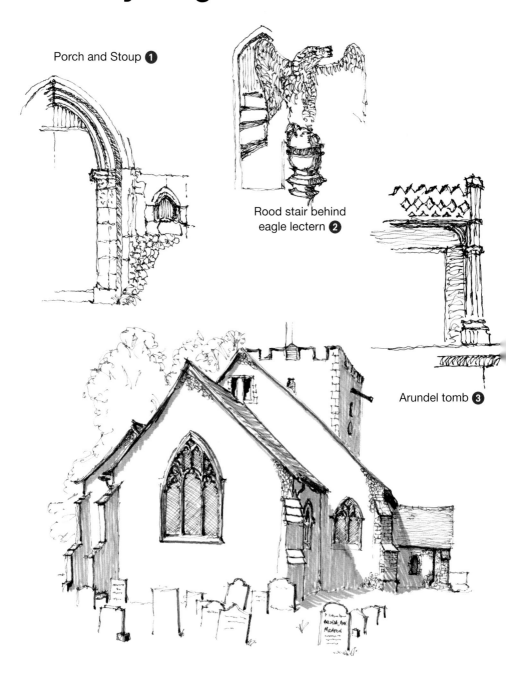

Porch and Stoup ❶

Rood stair behind
eagle lectern ❷

Arundel tomb ❸

What to look for:

1. As you approach the church there is a stoup to the right of the porch and a niche above the outer porch door probably for a St Mary statue. ❶

2. There is medieval graffiti in the north porch on the jambs of the doorway, with incised crosses, VV (Virgin of Virgins) and heraldic emblems including the ragged staff of the Earls of Warwick.

3. Rood stair: In the north-east corner of the nave, and in remarkable condition, with upper and lower openings. This must have given access to an impressive sizeable rood loft. ❷

4. Chancel: Along the north wall is a badly mutilated tomb thought to be that of the 10th Earl of Arundel, to its right is a square headed aumbry. There is also a medieval corbel on the north wall. Opposite, on the south wall to the right of the altar, is a 15th-century piscina and next to it the probable tomb of the 11th Earl of Arundel. ❸

5. The octagonal font is 15th-century.

6. High above the chancel arch, in the east gable, there's a window with a jumble of medieval glass put together to look like saints under canopies.

7. Do look at the epitaph to Thomas Johnson on the south aisle wall.

8. In the window of the east end of the north aisle is a lovely stained-glass window to the Blessed Virgin Mary made in 1979, and to the left is a statue to St Roche, the patron saint and healer of those stricken by the plague - when you leave Singleton and head to East Lavant you will climb the Trundle or St Roche's Hill, where there was a small chapel dedicated to St Roche until the 18th century.

Goodwood Racecourse

winter and early spring there is a ditch which you will need to cross via a narrow wooden bridge when there is running water. The path crosses a further stile and goes behind the Singleton Cricket Club pavilion to join the main road (A286). Be careful when crossing this busy main road and take the narrow side street 10 metres ahead on your right. Two hundred metres down this lane you will find The Partridge Inn on your left and a narrow lane to St Mary's church on your right.

Leave the church and turn left. Ahead at the fingerpost marked "The Trundle" turn left through the churchyard, you follow the line of the flint churchyard wall, keeping the massive square church tower on your left. Pass through a gate and across the farmyard where you will see, ahead of you, a finger post marked "public footpath" directing you straight uphill. Continue uphill and as you approach the crest you will see Goodwood Racecourse on your left.

The path merges onto a narrow metalled road, turn right and continue uphill for 500m to where the road merges with the busy road from Goodwood. There is a car park at the junction. Walk across the car park keeping to the left-hand side and cross the busy road at the place where you see steps going uphill. There is a fingerpost halfway up the steps on the right hand side pointing uphill. Take the path which

Chichester and the Solent from the Trundle

goes up a steep incline to The Trundle (from the Old English Tryndel meaning circle). The Trundle is the site of an Iron Age hill fort on top of St Roche's Hill:

https://en.wikipedia.org/wiki/The_Trundle

At the summit you pass through the fort gateway between the ramparts and continuing uphill you will see aerial masts on your right

St Mary East Lavant

Built in the 12th century it has been extensively remodelled, particularly during the Victorian period.

There is little to indicate the church is dedicated to St Mary, although there is a delightful small statue of Mary with the child Jesus on the window ledge of the bell tower, making this area suspended between Christ's birth and death, a wonderful and intimate potential Lady Chapel.

St Mary East Lavant

West door **1**

Tomb of Luci de Mildebi **2**

Misericord **3**

Easter Sepulchre **4**

What to look for:

1. The Norman west door has sculpted arches, chevrons, roll moulding and scallop capitals all made of locally quarried stone. ❶

2. The nave is original and is 12th century; the north aisle was added in the 13th century but was remodelled and extended along with the chancel in the 19th century.

3. The original north transept can be identified by the central two arches; one of the arches separating the nave and north aisle is original, as shown by a circular column between the second and third bays.

4. Medieval tomb slabs, one beneath the north arcade has indents for brass letters of a Lombardic inscription to Luci de Mildebi, asking us to pray for his (or possibly her) soul. There are references to Luci de Mildebi in local medieval documents relating to Manor Custumals, that is a list of duties for local parishioners, which means the family must have been a significant player in the local community. The other slab, which is less well preserved, is in the tower and was found in the chancel during its restoration. ❷

5. Chancel arch. It was rebuilt in 1863 but the core possibly retains some original medieval masonry, however there are no traces of any rood beam or screen.

6. Misericords. In the chancel stalls there are five 15th-century misericords. It is unusual to find these in a parish church, they are more commonly found in monasteries or priories. Their provenance is unknown, but as the church is in the gift of the Archbishop of Canterbury perhaps they were a presentation. ❸

7. Easter Sepulchre. Set within the bell tower is a medieval Easter Sepulchre which would originally have been in the north chancel wall. It was moved when the organ was installed. ❹

8. The small 12th-century south doorway, only uncovered in 1978, is next to the tower. The tower was rebuilt in 1671 and is thought to have replaced an earlier medieval tower, itself possibly built on the foundation of a south transept – the church may originally have had a cruciform shape.

and a path to the trig point on your left. Go to the trig point and admire the wonderful view – Chichester Cathedral due south with its copper roof and central tower, the expanse of Chichester Harbour with the Solent and Bembridge Cliffs on the Isle of Wight in the distance. Return to the path and cross to the other side of the fort, exit and continue downhill along the wide grass swathe with views across the Solent and, far to the west, Portsmouth, not far from your starting point in Portchester. You may be lucky enough see a Spitfire flying overhead from Goodwood aerodrome.

The grass swathe ends at a metalled road and nearby there is a large wooden fingerpost marked "St Roche's Hill". You follow the left-hand sign downhill to Lavant.

The path goes straight downhill and joins the road through East Lavant. Turn right and you soon pass the Royal Oak pub on your right – there is food and accommodation here – a further 200m on your right is the church of St Mary.

Take the road opposite the church (Fordwater Road) and after about 250m on your right there is a low flint walled barn. At the end of the flint wall you will see an unmarked path between a low hedge and field fence which avoids having to continue on this busy minor road. Take the path and after a little more than 100m on your right there is a gate and fingerpost directing you across the meadow. You cross a wooden bridge over the River Lavant and bear left, continue across the meadow and through a hawthorn hedge, then through another hedge where a fingerpost directs you straight onwards. Ahead of you is a long wooden garden fence where the path keeps to the left of the fence. Follow the path until it joins a narrow tarmacked lane, turn right – rejoining Fordwater Road.

You are now in the outskirts of Chichester and the lane widens to become a main thoroughfare of the built up area. You come to a T junction, turn left onto Summersdale Road. Walking on the roadside pavement you pass a long flint wall, the buildings behind used to be the quarters of the Royal Military Police but have been converted to housing. After ½ mile turn right into Wellington Road and shortly on the left-hand side is the car park for Oaklands Pavilion, the home of Chichester Rugby Football Club (CRFC). Pass by the pavilion onto the club rugby pitches which you keep on your right-hand side. The ground slopes down to the Festival Theatre. You can see the spire of Chichester Cathedral beyond.

Pass between the Festival and Minerva Theatres and into the theatre car park, walk directly across and take the subway under the roundabout which leads you to North Street. At the end of North Street is the Chichester Cross (built just before the Reformation) and turning right you will see the Cathedral on the left-hand side.
www.chichestercathedral.org.uk

Chichester Cathedral

The best way to visit the Cathedral is to take a guided tour, alternatively pick up the helpful leaflet which gives general information.

Construction of the magnificent Norman cathedral of Chichester began in the late 11th century under Bishop Stigand, a Norman who had replaced the Saxon Bishop Aethelric following the Conquest.

Imagine the Cathedral in the Medieval period, with its painted vault roof and pillars, a nave with no seating and numerous chapels – more than today – dedicated to individuals, families and local gilds. These chapels would have been separated by painted wooden screens with candles burning continuously and Mass being said for saints and the deceased at regular intervals.

Festival Theatre and Chichester Cathedral

Chichester Cathedral

Arundel screen ❶

Cathedral

Arundel tomb ❷

Market Cross

What to look for:

1. Arundel screen and loft, which has no obvious access apart from a modern metal stair but must have had a wooden or stone staircase originally to access a Rood. ❶

2. Choir stalls dating from 1315 which all have finely carved misericords.

3. The Romanesque 12th-century carvings depicting the "Raising of Lazarus".

4. The Arundel tomb, moved from Lewis Priory following its dissolution, made famous by Philip Larkin's poem – whose often quoted last line is "What will survive of us is love". ❷

5. The Cloister, at the western end, where there are medieval markings in the stone seating of a game played by waiting pilgrims – Nine Men's Morris.

6. Wall painting remains in the entrance arch to the Treasury and Gift Shop.

Lady Chapel

The original Lady Chapel was much smaller than the present Chapel, it was apsidal or semi-circular in shape, occupying the western end of the current chapel. It was one of three apsidal chapels radiating from the semi-circular ambulatory east of the choir.

The Lady Chapel was extended into a three bay chapel in the 12th century, possibly under Bishop Hilary (1147–1169) and finally remodelled as you see it today in the 13th century under Bishop Gilbert of St Leoford, who oversaw the transformation to the present "Decorated style". The small Norman windows at the western end were enlarged and new walls and windows were constructed giving the present Gothic tracery with pointed arches and foils.

Lady Chapel

Double piscina and three-step sedilia ❶

94

The Chapel fell into neglect following the Reformation and in 1780 was granted to the Duke of Richmond as a family mausoleum and had a major restoration in 1871.

The Chapel was refurbished in 2007 when some of the original colour incorporated into the fabric was discovered. This was reinstated as part of the restoration giving the bright vermillion and blue colouring on the vault ribs, along with the red and gold decoration on the bosses and capitals giving you an idea of how the whole Cathedral might have looked in the medieval period.

Today the chapel is set aside for private prayer, inviting you to sit and reflect on your four-day walk. Whilst resting you can observe the various medieval features:

What to look for:

1. The painted iron panels you enter through date from 1470, the gates however are a Victorian replica.

2. On the south wall near the altar a double piscina with a three-step sedilia just to their west, and a little further west is a double aumbry. The altar top or Mensa (Latin for table) is pre-Reformation, although the base is Victorian. ❶

3. Look at the vaulting at the western end of the chapel, the faded paintwork is by Bernard Lambert, a Renaissance Tudor painter (there are painted panels of national importance elsewhere in the Cathedral). This original paintwork only survived because the chapel was used as a library prior to becoming the Richmond mausoleum.

4. The bronze sculpture "Virgin and Child" was given by The Ecumenical Society of the Blessed Virgin Mary in 1988.

Finally

The first time I completed the full four-day walk I was accompanied by three friends. We collected cockle shells from the beach outside Portchester Castle and left them unobtrusively in the cloister garden of Chichester Cathedral – a memorial to our enjoyment and companionship throughout the journey.